FORD & FORDSON
TRACTORS

Robert N. Pripps and Andrew Morland

Motorbooks International
Publishers & Wholesalers ®

Dedication

...

For Hannah Morland

First published in 1995 by Motorbooks International Publishers & Wholesalers, PO Box 2, 729 Prospect Avenue, Osceola, WI 54020 USA

Library of Congress Cataloging-in-Publication Data
Morland, Andrew.
    Ford & Fordson tractors / Andrew Morland.
    Robert Pripps.
      p. cm. -- (Motorbooks International enthusiast color series)
    Includes index.
    ISBN 0-7603-0044-5 (pbk.)
    1. Ford tractors--History. 2. Fordson tractors--History.
    I. Pripps, Robert N., 1932- II. Title. III. Series: Enthusiast color series.
    TL233.5.M67   1995   95-14011
    629.225--dc20

On the front cover: The 1956 Ford 650 was one of the three variations on the 600 series tractor. *Andrew Morland*

On the frontispiece: A 1953 Ford Golden Jubilee with owner and restorer Norm Seveik and son Jeremy at the controls. *Andrew Morland*

On the title page: A 1939 Ford-Ferguson 9N with aluminum hood and grille. *Andrew Morland*

On the back cover: A 1932 Ford 8N with a Funk Ford V-8 conversion. Palmer Fossum is at the controls. *Andrew Morland*

Printed in Hong Kong

Contents

Acknowledgments

This book could not have been put together without the help and co-operation of the Ford and Fordson owners in North America and in Great Britain. A special thank you goes to the following enthusiastic owners:

Don Alstead, John Davis, Brian Brekken, Marlo Remme, Norm Seveik in the U.S.A.; John Carwood, Tom Hooper, John Turner, Tony Rossiter, Jeremy Ellis, Keith Dorey, and John Lock in Great Britain.

Also to:

Daniel Zilm, Fordson new parts and mechanical restorations (R.R. 1, Box 242, Claremont, MN 55924).

Duane Helman, new parts manufacturer for Fordson (Rosewood Machine and Tool Co., Box 17, Rosewood, OH 43070)

Gene H. Hemphill, (Manager, Industry Affairs, Ford New Holland, Inc.)

Palmer Fossum, Ford parts and restoration (10201E 100th Street Northfield, MN 55057). The Old Twenty Parts Company, spare parts for Ford, Fordson, and Fordson Majors Cavendish Bridge, (Shardlow, Nr. Derby, DE72 2HL Great Britain).

The Henry Ford Museum, Greenfield Village, Detroit, Michigan.

Paul Browne of New Holland Ford Ltd., who was extremely efficient and helpful.

Margaret Loula and Peter Olsen of the Ford Motor Company, for providing the latest Ford Ranger Splash Pickup for my travels with Bob Pripps in our pursuit of restored Ford and Fordson tractors.

A final and particular thank you to Robert Pripps, the renowned Ford tractor expert, for agreeing to write this book.

Foreword

Henry Ford did more than put the world on wheels; he changed the way people lived. If this was true for the automobile and the general public, it was even more true for tractors and the farmer. Tractors by Ford have continuously shaped the rest of the market. Ford tractors have held a major share of the world's tractor market since 1918; much of the time in the early days, seventy percent of the market. Today, Ford tractors are number one in worldwide sales.

To most people, be they city or country, the name "Ford tractor" conjures a vision of a squat, small, gray machine that touched their lives somewhere along the way. For more than the last half of the seventy-seven-year history of Ford-built tractors, however, they have been painted blue, rather than gray. And the product line includes not just one type, but tractors ranging from riding mowers to articulated four-wheel drive monsters.

The first production Ford tractor rolled out the factory door in 1917. In 1995, although the name is still on the product, Ford Motor Company is no longer involved. Ford tractors are a product of New Holland N.V. which was formed in 1991 by the merger of Fiat S.p.A.'s Fiatgeotech and Ford-New Holland's agricultural and construction machinery interests. In the merger, Ford retained a twenty percent interest. By the end of 1993, however, Ford sold it's remaining stock and the company was 100 percent owned by Fiat S.p.A.

Apparently, the current Ford Motor Company management did not share old Henry's interest in farming. More importantly, they likely did not share his lack of interest in tractor profits. Back in 1939, Henry made the altruistic statement to the press that he didn't care to make a profit on the tractor, "I'm going the limit to help my country," he said.

The photos in this book show the tractors that revolutionized the industry and forced much of its progress. They are interspersed with text that covers the history of the various models along with some technical descriptions and specifications. Our thanks to those who allowed us to photograph their restored antiques and to those who interrupted their farming long enough for us to get photos of their machinery.

Andrew Morland
Robert Pripps

Chapter One

Henry Ford and the Ford Motor Company

The formation of The Ford Motor Company in 1903, and its impact on the automobile world, are a well understood part of history. Also historically important, though not so apparent, is Henry Ford's role in the development of the farm tractor. Tractors by Ford have been used in great numbers all over the world since 1918. The tractors have been technological trend-setters since the beginning. In the early days, they were instrumental in farm mechanization.

Henry Ford was the oldest child of William and Mary Ford. William had emigrated from the Cork area of Ireland to Dearborn, Michigan. By the time Henry was born in 1863, his father had a substantial farm of several hundred acres. Naturally, young Henry was pressed into the farm duties.

From early on, young Henry Ford did not take to the job of farming. He would later write, "There was just too much work around the place." As soon as he was old enough, he left for Detroit and a job building streetcars with the Michigan Car Company. The hard manual labor of the farm did, nevertheless, spawn his interest in reducing the farmer's burden with mechanical devices. While still on the farm, he became enamored with steam power and steam engines, and he became quite adept at their operation and repair.

Henry also became quite skilled at watch repair, claiming the he had fixed his first watch at age thirteen, after making his own tools for the repair. This skill helped him make a living while getting started in Detroit.

When Henry Ford turned twenty-one, his father gave him a wooded forty acres of the farm. It was a blatant effort on the part of the senior Ford to entice the younger Ford back to Dearborn. Henry did return and lived on the property for five years. During that time, he set up a saw mill, logged the property, sold the lumber, and returned to Detroit.

In the intervening years, he had been called upon many times to repair Otto-cycle (four-cycle) engines. In the late 1880s, this new type engine was in its infancy. Henry soon became an expert, and began designing his own soon after returning to Detroit. In 1893, the same year Henry and his wife, Clara, had their only child, Edsel, Henry's first ever gasoline engine burst into life, clamped to the kitchen sink. By 1896, Ford's "Quadricycle" automobile was a familiar sight on the Detroit streets.

There were to be two failed automotive ventures in Henry Ford's life before the foundation of the Ford Motor Company in 1903. The first was the Detroit Automobile Company, the second was called the Henry Ford Company. Finally, with the help of influential investors, the Ford Motor Company was founded. This company

A 1907 Ford automobile plow. Joseph Galamb developed this experimental tractor for Henry Ford. The 1,500lb tractor was powered by a 24hp Ford transversely mounted four-cylinder engine. This one is displayed at the Henry Ford Museum, Detroit.

had the talent and resources to get into volume production, and by 1906, production was up to 100 cars per day.

Ford and Tractors

In 1906, Ford's interest returned to farming and he began the first of many tractor experiments. When asked by an interviewer about his tractor interests, he said that his aim was to make farming what it ought to be, the most pleasant and profitable profession in the world. Some will question whether his dream was ever realized; others will question whether Henry Ford's tractors, at least the early ones, contributed to making farming pleasant and profitable. Nevertheless, the tractors that resulted from Ford's early experiments left an indelible mark on farming. The first of these was the Fordson.

Chapter Two

The Fordson

The Fordson Model F

The Fordson had its roots in World War I. A Ford engineer named Eugene Farkas had designed a four-wheel, four-cylinder, three-speed machine which featured a worm drive reduction gear into the differential. It also featured a frame-less structure, whereby the engine and transmission and differential housings acted as the frame of the tractor.

By 1916, the British were engaged in the war and were becoming concerned about food production, what with the demands of the war for men and horses, and the possibility of disrupted foreign supply. It was then that the Farkas-designed tractor was demonstrated to the British. The machines impressed British government officials and led to an immediate order of 6,000 of the tractors for British production. The order was placed by the Ministry of Munitions (MOM) and the tractors supplied under this order became known as MOM tractors.

The Ministry of Munitions expected Ford's British company to make the tractors in

This 1918 Fordson Model F was photographed outside Duane Helman's Tractor Workshops in Rosewood, Ohio. Helman's Rosewood Machine and Tool Co. produce many new parts for Ford and Fordson tractors.

England. Because he felt he owed something to his roots, Henry Ford, however, decided to set up the factory in Cork, Ireland, from whence the Ford family emigrated. Production was not in Cork until after the war, however, as resources were in too short supply in Britain and the need for the tractors was too great.

Between the time the order was accepted and when production started the design was given an overhaul. As many as 15 X-models were built and tested, each X-model being progressively more like the production tractor. In the process the car-type radiator was increased in size so that its capacity was eleven gallons to cure overheating problems. The additional weight also helped hold the front down. Next, the worm drive in the rear end was relocated. It had been on top, under the seat. During heavy operation the heat became unbearable to the operator. Revising the design to put the worm below solved the problem of the hot seat and also allowed larger rear wheels. Thus another problem was overcome, that of inadequate traction. Finally several changes were made to simplify manufacture. The Fordson would use the Model T coil magneto system. Water and oil pumps would be eliminated in favor of the simpler thermocycle cooling and splash lubrication.

Ford prototype number X-9 of 1916. The four-cylinder 251ci engine was built by Hercules and outfitted with a Holley carburetor and manifold for Ford Motor Co. Owner Duane Helman

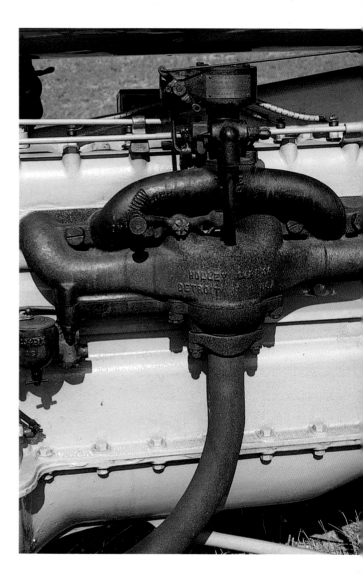

Before the end of 1917, 254 MOM tractors were completed. Tractors were not formally called Fordsons until the MOM order was completed and production for the general public started.

Production problems plagued the new assembly line at the Dearborn plant and deliveries were way behind schedule. Nevertheless, production got on track in 1918. The 6,000 tractors amounted to less than sixty days of production, although actual deliveries took somewhat longer. Because of shipping limitations, many were not delivered to England, but to Canada and other Commonwealth locations. The balance of the MOM order was then filled by production Fordsons.

Henry Ford set up a new and separate company to build these tractors. The Ford Motor Company was still a stockholder-owned company at this time, and Henry chafed under the restrictions and control of the "board." Taking his now twenty-three-year-old son, Edsel, in with him, Henry called the new company "Henry Ford and Son." Later, in communicating via the transatlantic cable, the name was abbreviated to "Fordson", and that name was used for the tractor when it went into production after the M.O.M. order was completed.

By mid-1918, more than 6,000 little gray tractors were farming in Britain, Canada, and the United States. After World War I was over, production began in Cork in parallel to U.S. production.

Fordsons, now designated as the Model F, were produced in the U.S and Ireland in great

Right: The 1916 prototype Fordson shows the simple, revolutionary design. Eugene Farkas successfully made the engine, gearbox, and rear axle a stressed member of the frame. By eliminating the need for a heavy, separate frame, this saved costs and simplified manufacturing. Farkas and Ford must have been heavily influenced, however, by the only other tractor to use this unit frame, the Wallis Cub, which was built in 1913.

numbers. Production eclipsed that of all the other tractor makers with Ford holding seventy percent of the world's market.

Towards the end of 1919, Henry Ford established the Eastern Holding Company, a Delaware corporation, for the purpose of bringing

lion, Eastern Holding procured the assets of the Ford Motor Company, Henry Ford & Son, Inc., and some other of Ford's business interests. In early 1920, when these activities were completed, the Eastern Holding name was dropped in favor of the Michigan-chartered Ford Motor Company.

Now freed of stockholder control, Henry Ford was able to move toward his goal of manufacturing vehicles from raw materials, rather than by purchasing sub-assemblies from suppliers. One of his first moves was the construction of the giant River Rouge plant, outside Detroit.

The Rouge plant contained its own power house, steel smelting plant, and ship-docking facility. Fordson production was terminated at the Brady Street plant in Dearborn and transferred to the new Rouge plant. From the 1920 model and on, the stamping on the end of the fuel tank reads "Manufactured by Ford Motor Company, Detroit, Michigan (or Cork, Ireland)."

When production was up to speed at the River Rouge plant in 1922, production was discontinued at the Cork, Ireland plant and at the newly instituted Hamilton, Ohio plant. At its lowest point (in 1922), the price of the Fordson dropped to $395.

A transmission brake was added in 1923. An aftermarket parts business flourished at this time, providing parts, it was said, that Ford would not. High-compression heads, gasoline manifolds, and water pumps were

company control back to the family by acquiring all the minority stock in the Ford Motor Company. With family capital of over $100 mil-

A Fordson Model F built in 1918. Hannah Morland is at the controls of Daniel Zilm's perfectly restored tractor. The F was listed as a 10–20hp tractor, but in Great Britain it was marketed as an 18hp. This Model F is fitted with Ford supplied W & K wheels and runs on number one fuel oil (similar to kerosene).

available, as were crawler tracks. Ford did provide a hard rubber-tired industrial Fordson, however.

The Fordson tractor was essentially a mature item by 1924. The Ford Motor Company was also hitting its stride by that year, the financial troubles of 1921 and 1922 behind them. In fact, 1923 Fordson production had set a record for tractor production of 101,898 units (surpassed only by Fordson in 1925). In 1924, 900 Fordsons were sent to the Soviet Union. Eventually, some 25,000 would follow. During 1925, the 500,000th Fordson was built and an unsurpassed tractor model production record of 104,168 was set.

In 1924, the appearance of the Fordson was changed by the use of a lighter gray paint and by the availability of optional fenders. In 1925,

A 1918 Fordson Model F. The four-cylinder L-head engine produced 20hp at the belt pulley and 10hp at the drawbar. In the United States the 4in bore and 5in stroke Model F was rated at 20.19hp. Fifty percent of the engine power was lost, however, through the gears and worm wheel differential, so that only 10hp was produced at the rear wheels. The owner is Daniel Zilm.

tool-box fenders, sometimes called orchard fenders, were made available. Besides a handy place to store tools, these fenders were supposed to prevent rearing accidents for which Fordsons were becoming infamous.

The Fordson was always hard to start unless the ignition system was perfect (which it seldom was). Crank kicks were notorious for breaking the arm of the cranker. Once operating, the Fordson was singularly noisy. The straight (unmuffled) exhaust pipe exited under the seat, and the worm drive made a howl that could be heard for miles!

The Fordson worked extremely well on the belt. When using the drawbar, however, the inefficiency of the worm drive sapped a full one-half of the power (hence the heat under the seat). Nevertheless, it was as good at pulling a plow as

A 1926 Fordson Model F, serial number 583701. The four-cylinder engine with a bore of 4in and 5in stroke produced 20.19hp at the belt on gasoline. Extras fitted to this F include Pierce governor, 1934 French & Hecht wheels, and a water pump. The owner is Daniel Zilm.

any other 10hp drawbar-rated tractor. Steering was much better than many, due to the automobile influence. The short wheelbase aided maneuverability but led to the danger of rearing accidents. All tractors will go over backwards given the right (wrong) conditions, but the Fordson did it quicker and more often, leading to more than 200 deaths by 1925. The long-tail fenders were designed to pop the wheel lugs out of the ground to allow slippage, but they didn't always work.

Also in 1925 and 1926, more aftermarket variations on the Fordson theme appeared. There were graders, road rollers, golf course mowers, and the like.

By 1927, the Fordson's U.S. production days were numbered. Nevertheless, the Fordson enjoyed a good year with production (which actually ended in 1928) of over 100,000 units. Approximately 8,000 of these were built in what would be the 1928 model

Above: A 1925 Fordson Model F. The wire from the flywheel and ignition box containing the troublesome vibrator or trembler coil can be seen on the 20hp engine. The owner is Russell Schafer from Michigan.

Right: A 1926 Fordson Model F. The rear fenders with the enclosed tool boxes were designed to slow down the back flips that were common on Fordsons when plowing. This disturbing tendency was due to the tractor's rear weight bias, which unfortunately did not help traction. The Fordson always produced the lowest traction efficiency in tests on both sides of the Atlantic.

This Fordson Model N row crop serial number 831504 was built in 1938, the last year Fordsons were imported to the United States. The tractor is equipped with French and Hecht wheels, Bosch FU4 magneto, and Plymouth pulley. The owner is Daniel Zilm.

year, but most consider them late-built 1927 models.

The new Model A Ford car was to be built on such a scale that the production facilities of the Fordson tractor were needed. Ford could also see that the American farmer's appetite for tractors was changing. The Farmall introduced in 1924 had revolutionized their thinking just as the Fordson had in 1917. Ford realized that his profit potential would be continuously squeezed by these new competitive row-crop tractors unless he undertook a new design, but he had his hands full with the new car and truck line.

In December of 1928 Ford transferred control of Ford Motor Company, (England) Ltd. and Henry Ford & Son, Ltd. of Cork, to British citizens and to a new company, Ford Motor

Company, Ltd. Worldwide rights to the Fordson tractor were assigned to the new company. In 1928, all production tooling was transferred to Cork, where production had been discontinued previously in 1922. So, in 1928, production of the Fordson in the United States was discontinued.

Characteristics of the Fordson F

Engine: Hercules-built, 4x5in bore and stroke, 251cid, four-cylinder, L-head, rated at 1000rpm. Ford-built after 1920, but essentially the same unit.

Weight: 2,710 pounds initially, growing to 3,000 pounds

Transmission: three speeds forward, one reverse

Final Drive: Worm and wheel

Color: Gray with bright red wheels, no fenders until 1925

Brakes: None until 1923, then a transmission disk brake clutch pedal-operated. Indus-trial version available with pneumatic tires and wheel brakes in 1927.

British Fordsons

The Fordson Model N

Fordsons were built in Cork from 1928 to 1933. The most important change made for the Irish N was in the engine. First, the bore was increased 0.125in, bumping displacement to 267cid, rather than the 251ci of the Fordson F. Next, a high-tension impulse-coupling conventional magneto replaced the Model T coils. The performance of aftermarket high-compression

A radiator from a 1938 Fordson Model N. The ribbed radiator top tank appeared in 1932 on the blue Model Ns. The Model N was rated as a 12–23hp from the 267ci four-cylinder engine.

gasoline heads did not go unnoticed, and Ford offered a gasoline version with a high-compression head. The new Model N was available in either kerosene or gasoline versions. The University of Nebraska's typically conservative ratings for the two versions of the Model N were: 21hp (kerosene) and 26hp (gasoline) on the belt.

Instead of spoked front wheels, the new Model N had cast front wheels. It also had a heavier front axle with a downward bend in the middle and a larger water-washer air cleaner. The paint scheme remained the same, but the wing-type "orchard" fenders were standard. On the rear end of the fuel tank were the words "Ford Motor Company, Ltd., England, Made in Irish Free State." Some said "Made by Ford Motor Company, Ltd., Cork, Ireland."

In 1933, production transferred to Ford Motor Company, Ltd., of Dagenham, England. At the time of the transfer the venerable Fordson was given a facelift. This included a striking blue

Left: The 1938 Fordson Model N row crop was marketed in the United States as the "Fordson All-Around." The Fordson design was twenty-one years old by 1938, and the tractor built in Dagenham, Great Britain had less than five percent of the American market. The owner is Marlo Remme, Dennison, MN.

paint job, conventional fenders with the tool box on the dash, a ribbed pattern cast into the radiator tank, and the Fordson name cast in the radiator side panels. The fuel tank end now said "Ford Motor Company, Ltd., Made in England."

A 1938 Fordson Model N row crop (also known as the Fordson All-Around). The Dagenham British built four-cylinder L-head produced over 29hp at the belt on gasoline at the Nebraska tests. This nicely restored Model N is owned by Daniel Zilm of Claremont, MN.

The 1942 Fordson Model N with a popular postwar Perkins L-4 diesel engine conversion. These engine transplants extended the life of the Model N, giving a large increase of power and better fuel consumption. The four-cylinder diesel produced 45bhp at 1500rpm from 270ci.

The Fordson was again modernized in 1935 with pneumatic tires, lights, power take-off, and bright orange trim on the blue paint. In 1937, flagging U.S. import sales prompted another update; the tricycle-configured Fordson All-Around. It was given a bright new orange paint job, an oil-bath air cleaner, and higher compression heads for both the gas and distillate models.

Production of the Model N continued into 1945. During the war years, however, the orange paint was switched to a more subdued, and less visible-to-enemy-aircraft green.

The Fordson Model E27N Major

Following the war years, the Fordson was upgraded again and dubbed the Model E27N. The new version featured increased ground clearance (useful for cultivating) and would be capable of pulling a three-bottom plow. Since the original worm drive would not take the additional load, a redesigned rear axle with a spiral bevel drive and bull gears was incorporated. The new rear axle, combined with a downward-extending king-pin front axle, gave the new E27N the desired higher stance.

The new design worked well, except for the thirty-year-old engine. Now rated at 27hp, instead of its original 20hp, the engine was not noted for its long life. This was soon remedied by installation of a Perkins diesel

A 1941 Fordson Model N built at Dagenham. The factory on the River Thames, near London, was bombed many times by the Germans, but production of the Model N only ended in 1945 when the E27N model went into production. A horse-drawn Somerset root drill of 1937 is being used. The owner is Robin Symonds.

engine. Some 23,000 E27N Major diesels were delivered by the time production ended in 1952.

Fordson New Major, Power Major, Super Major

Next came the Fordson New Major, Power Major, and Super Major. These were modern and competitive conventional tractors. Eventually, about ninety percent were powered by a Ford-designed diesel. Three engines were used. Early versions were 199ci units that shared the same block and crank. Compression ratios were 4.35:1 for tractor vaporizing oil (TVO), 5.5:1 for gasoline, and 16:1 for the diesel. The later versions, the Power Major and Super Major, featured horsepower in-

A Fordson Major built on February 2nd, 1952, with gasoline/kerosene engine and no hydraulics. The owner is John Turner of Grateley, Great Britain, plowing with three-furrow Cockshutt plow at the Dorset Steam Fair, Dorset, Great Britain.

creases, and diesel versions had a displacement advantage (to 220cid) over the gasoline and TVO versions.

The new tractor was much larger and heavier than the E27N, weighing in at about 5,300 pounds. It used a three-speed transmission with a two-range shifter, giving it six forward speeds and two in reverse. It had a hydraulic power lift, a twelve-volt electrical system, and power steering was available. Fordson Super Majors were imported to the U.S. The imported models were painted beige with blue trim rather than just blue and were labeled the Ford 5000. Production continued through 1962, when Ford consolidated its worldwide tractor operations.

The Fordson Dexta and Super Dexta

The year 1957 marked Ford of U.K.'s return to the compact tractor market. The new 3,000lb Dexta had a squat, low stance, and a low center of gravity. It was rated at 32hp and had a hydraulic three-point hitch.

The Dexta used a 144ci three-cylinder Perkins diesel engine. It was coupled to a three-speed with a two-range gearbox giving six speeds forward and two in reverse. Live power take-off (PTO) and hydraulics were options. The Dexta could handle a three-bottom plow in most soils. The hydraulic controls were designed to accommodate remote double-acting cylinders as well as the three-point hitch.

The Fordson Dexta was built in Dagenham, Great Britain from 1958–61. The Super Dexta was built from 1962–64. Dexta was powered by a 144ci three-cylinder Perkins diesel engine that was rated at 32hp. This 1960 model is owned by Randall Olson of Pecatonica, Illinois.

Left top: A 1964 Fordson Major built in Dagenham with the Ford 219ci diesel engine. This model is known as a Rice Field Special. These high-crop conversions were done by Ford dealers in the Southern States for sugar cane or rice farming. This one will be restored by owner Palmer Fossum.

Left bottom: A Fordson Super Major Triple-D (DOE Dual Drive) built in 1962 at Maldon, Essex, Great Britain. Popular on the large farms of Lincolnshire and Norfolk, Great Britain. The Triple-D is two Fordson Majors joined together to make a four-wheel-drive articulated tractor with a total 439ci of diesel power. Owned and restored by John Hooper, Dorset, Great Britain.

The Dexta used adjustable-length front axles. The rear wheel width was power-adjustable.

The Super Dexta, introduced in 1962, had a displacement increase to 153cid, and an increase in rated RPM. Between 1962 and 1964, the Super Dexta was imported to the U.S. as the Ford 2000 Diesel.

A Fordson E27N Major Roadless Model E with Fordson four-cylinder L-head engine equipped to burn TVO (Tractor Vaporizing Oil). Only twenty-five E27N Majors were converted by Roadless. Photographed at the Great Dorset Steam Fair, Blandford, Dorset, Great Britain.

Left: A 1948 Fordson E27N Major built in Dagenham, Great Britain outfitted with. a Perkins L-4 four-cylinder diesel. The 270ci engine put out 45hp at 1500rpm with 182lb-ft torque at 1000rpm from the long stroke 4.75in and 4.5in bore. These conversions made Perkins prosperous and transformed the E27N. The owner is Tony Rossiter, Meare, Great Britain.

Below; A 1949 Fordson Major E27N model with P-6 Perkins diesel engine. The Perkins six-cylinder engine was a production Fordson option after 1948. Perkins also offered engine conversions to install their L-4 and P-6 diesels. The P-6 produced the same power as the L-4— 45bhp at 1500rpm—but was much smoother. The L-6 had a bore of 3.5in and stroke of 5in and displaced 289ci. The engine was in a low, unstressed state of tune as the road-going commercial version of the P-6 produced 73bhp at 2400rpm. The owner is M.G. Turner, Wimborne, Dorset, Great Britain.

A 1952 Ford 8N with Funk V8 conversion. Palmer Fossum plowing with his rare tractor. Most Funk 8N conversions used the six-cylinder industrial or truck Ford engine. Note the two vertical exhaust pipes.

Chapter Three

The N Series

Ford-Ferguson

Irishman Harry Ferguson, a charismatic inventor and manufacturer of farm machinery, had contrived the three-point implement system with automatic compensation for changing draft loads. Ferguson had gone into business with the English manufacturer, David Brown, to build a small Fordson-like tractor called the Ferguson-Brown, which incorporated the new hydraulic three-point hitch. Poor economic conditions in the early thirties, plus high prices, left the Ferguson-Brown company foundering. Brown and Ferguson got into a dispute over what to do to increase sales to a profitable level and eventually parted ways. Ferguson demonstrated the tractor and integral implements to Henry Ford at Ford's Fair Lane estate. When the Ferguson-Brown out-plowed a Fordson and several other brands of tractors Ford had on the place, Henry Ford struck a gentleman's agreement with Ferguson on the spot to build a new tractor incorporating the Ferguson "system."

After less than a year of design and development, in June of 1939, the new Ford-Ferguson 9N was unveiled for the press. The tractor was an immediate success with more than 10,000 being sold yet that year.

The new tractor was designated the 9N: 9 for the year 1939; N the Ford designation for tractor. It was a vast improvement over the both the Fordson and the Ferguson-Brown. It retained the unified frame-less structure of its predecessors but used what has become known as the "utility tractor front axle." This is a straight axle, pivoted in the center and with downward-extending king-pins. With this arrangement, more crop clearance is obtained, and the tractor is given a higher roll center, for greater stability.

Henry Ford's main objective was an affordable cost. Early on, he established a selling price goal of less than $600, believing such a price would result in sufficient demand to meet his production goal of 1,000 units per week. That would be enough to keep an assembly line busy. To meet the cost objective, many parts from the car and truck lines were adapted. For example, the 119.5ci four-cylinder engine was half of the 239ci V-8 used in cars and trucks.

Styling was a big factor in tractors in 1939. The Ford styling department took on the 9N, and the result was an absolutely perfect blend of art deco flair and producibility. The styling was so good that Ford changed it very little for the next thirteen years.

A 1948 Ford 8N with a Bombardier half-track kit, which could be used for field work, but was designed for snow or mud. The Bombardier Company of Valcourt, Quebec is still in business today building Ski-Doo snowmobiles amd Camadaor aircraft.

Fenders were standard equipment, as was the self-starter. Lights were optional, but a PTO and reverse-flow muffler were standard.

Almost all domestic 9Ns were made to run on gasoline only, but a variation, the 9NAN, used distillate. Most 9NANs were exported, many finding their way to Great Britain. The 9NAN was fitted with a Holley Vaporizer like the one used on the Fordson F.

What made the 9N Ford-Ferguson unique, however, was the Ferguson System; the load-compensating system of mounted implements and the hydraulic three-point hitch. The tractor had an internal hydraulic system that raised or lowered the implement via two lower mounting links. A semi-parallel upper link was connected to a hydraulic control valve through a stiff coil spring. Once the operator set the implement,

A 1948 Ford 8N with Bombardier half-tracks. The 119.7ci four-cylinder engine was one half of the 239ci V-8 car and truck engine. The owner is Palmer Fossum of Northfield, MN.

such as a plow, to the desired depth, the reaction of loads through the upper link caused the system to raise the plow in more difficult soil in order to maintain a constant draft load. Once the hard spot was passed, the implement automatically returned to the preset depth. The act of raising the plow also caused downforce on the rear wheels, preventing wheel slip. More importantly, the action of the top link prevented rearing accidents for which the Fordsons had become infamous.

Ford Motor Company built the tractor and sold it to a marketing company set up by Ferguson. This company sold the tractors and implements to the users. Included were the Sherman Brothers, friends of Henry Ford who had been importers of the Fordson N. The new company was called Ferguson-Sherman Manufacturing Corporation. Ferguson-Sherman also designed and built a line of custom implements. The implement line eventually grew to around 400 implements.

The Ford-Ferguson 2N

Shortages and restrictions of World War II began to impact production of the 9N. Therefore, a simplified version was introduced, which had no starter, generator, or lights. It was also equipped with steel wheels, rather than rubber tires. The designation was changed from 9N to 2N (for 1942) to reflect the changes and also, a new model was not so definitely tied to the old

A 1939 Ford-Ferguson 9N, serial number 357, with noted Ford author Bob Pripps at the controls. Note the unusual horizontal grill holes. Aluminum grilles and hoods were used on tractors that were built before the steel parts were ready.

for War Production Board controls which fixed prices. By calling the 2N a new model, prices could be raised.

As time went on, however, the starter, generator, and lights, along with the rubber tires, found their way back and except for minor year-by-year changes, the 2N was much the same as the 9N. The Model 2N was produced until mid-1947.

In 1946, with young Henry Ford II in control of The Ford Motor Company, Ferguson was told that the deal was over. Young Henry had discovered that Ferguson was the only partner in the deal that had made any money and, therefore, wanted to end the arrangement. Ford was building the tractors for Ferguson at a fixed price, and Ferguson sold the tractors and equipment to the farmers through Ferguson dealers.

This was the final blow for Harry Ferguson. He had expected that, in 1939, the British Ford Motor Company, Ltd. would begin making the

A 1941 Ford-Ferguson 9N. Marketed as a Ford tractor with the Ferguson system and later as the Ford-Ferguson. Some say Harry Ferguson insisted on having his name on the tractor, others contend that Henry Ford insisted that the Ferguson name be displayed. Note that the grill is incorrect for a 1941 model.

Ford-Ferguson and drop the Fordson so that he could also sell to the European market. That, however, was not to happen. Instead, his market was now shrinking. Ferguson had set up his own tractor manufacturing arrangement in England when it became apparent that Fordson production would continue and started produc-

ing an improved version of the 9N, which he called the Ferguson TE-20.

In the meantime, Ford engineers began work on a replacement for the Ford-Ferguson.

The Ford 8N

On September 5, 1946, the Ford Motor Company announced that after the next June 30, it would discontinue the manufacture of the tractor for Harry Ferguson, Inc. and would build an improved tractor for distribution through independent dealers.

Ford then began construction of a completely new model (although it looked much the same) called the 8N for introduction in the 1948 model year. Ford also designed and built its own complete line of implements and set up its own dealer network. Ferguson had already began production of his own look-alike tractor in England, called the Ferguson TE-20. In order to supply his dealers, Ferguson began importing the TE-20 to the U.S. He also set up a factory in Detroit to build an American version called the TO-20.

On November 26, 1946, about two weeks after Harry Ferguson was notified that the agreement was to be discontinued, Henry Ford II announced the formation of Dearborn Motors to market a new tractor model. Dearborn was to design and build a completely new line of implements, as well.

Harry Ferguson then brought suit against the Ford Motor Company for $251 million. He charged patent infringement and loss of business, because Ford quit supplying tractors.

The real bone of contention was the hydraulic control system, which regulated flow by restricting the supply-side of the pump. Ford en-

A 1939 Ford-Ferguson 9N with aluminum hood
and grille. The four-cylinder L-head Ford
119.7ci engine produced 28hp at 2000rpm.

gineers had always considered that to be the hard way to do the job but didn't have time to change it for the 8N. This was the only point on which Ferguson won. In an out-of-court settlement approved by the court, Ford was instructed to stop using supply-side control by the end of the 1952 model year. The success of Ferguson's TO-20 tractor belied loss of business damages. The settlement was for $9.25 million, a fraction of the amount Ford had spent in its defense.

In July of that year, the 8N tractor and implements were ready. Model 2N production stopped and 8N production took over. The farmers' enthusiastic reception of the tractor made 1947 the best year for tractor production in twenty years.

Rather than the machinery forest gray of the 9N-2N, the 8N's sheet metal was painted light gray and the cast iron was painted red. The tractor was, however, the same size and shape as the 9N and 2N. It also used the same engine, although the compression ratio was raised slightly during production. The hydraulic three-point hitch was improved, and a new four-speed transmission replaced the three-speed version. Also, the 8N's brake pedals were both on the right side, rather than one on each side as they had been on previous models.

Production of the 8N continued through 1952, when the hydraulic system was changed to comply with the court's mandate. The 8N became Ford's second largest-selling tractor model, after the Fordson F.

The NAA Jubilee

The Ferguson suit forced Ford to redesign the hydraulic system after 1952. Therefore, they decided to upgrade the whole tractor. For the

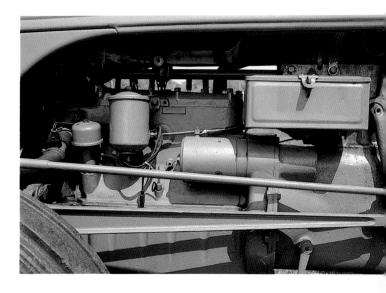

A 1940 Ford-Ferguson 9N. The Ford L-head four-cylinder engine has a 3.187 x 3.75in bore and stroke to give total displacement of 119.7ci. twenty-four hp is produced at the belt pulley but the engine is rated at twenty-eight hp.

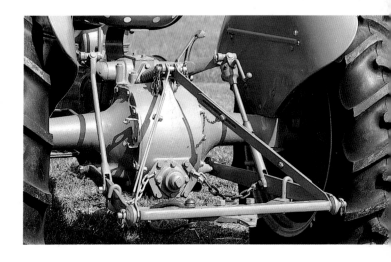

A 1940 Ford-Ferguson 9N. The 9N was equipped with Harry Ferguson's three-point hitch, which first appeared as the Ferguson "Black Tractor" back in 1933.

A 1952 Ford 8N with a Funk Ford V-8 conversion by Funk Brothers of Coffeeville, Kansas, who were well known for their light aircraft. Palmer Fossum is at the controls adjusting the depth of the plow and trying to reduce tire slip with the 239ci engine in a 2700lb tractor.

Golden Jubilee Fiftieth Anniversary of Ford Motor Company in 1953, Ford brought out the Model NAA Jubilee.

Production of the new Jubilee began in January of 1953. It was larger and heavier and sported a totally new overhead-valve four-cylinder 134ci engine. Also, it was completely restyled so that it no longer resembled previous Ford tractors or the Ferguson TO-30, which came out in 1951, and was stiff competition for the 8N.

A new "live" or direct engine-driven hydraulic pump and system was incorporated, eliminating conflict with the Ferguson patents. Originally, a vane pump was used, mounted under the hood along side the engine. Later, a piston-type pump was substituted. A separate hydraulic reservoir was provided, as were provisions for remote hydraulic cylinders.

A non-live PTO was standard on the Jubilee, but a live PTO was offered as an option.

The Jubilee also had improved brakes and rear axle seals and an improved governor. The muffler was relocated from below the engine to under the hood. This reduced the possibility of the muffler causing fires in dry straw, and also allowed for optional vertical exhausts. The instrument panel now contained a temperature gauge as standard equipment.

The 1954 version can be distinguished from the 1953 model by their revised star-en-

A 1952 Ford 8N with Funk Ford V-8 conversion. The tractor was lengthened and the tie and radius rods were extended. An instrument panel extends the hood which is also raised with the grille. Gearbox adapters and a bigger radiator complete the Funk package (mufflers are optional)! Owner and restorer Palmer Fossum is at the controls.

circled nose medallion rather than the one that had the words "Golden Jubilee Model 1903-1953." Internally, the 1954 version had gear ratio changes which reduced operating speed for a given engine RPM to increase drawbar pull.

Jubilee tractors were painted red and gray, the same as the 8Ns.

Above: A 1952 Ford 8N fitted with vee snow plow. The 2410lb tractor is powered by a four-cylinder 119.5ci engine with a compression ratio of 6.5:1.

Left: A 1952 Ford 8N with Funk V-8 conversion. Note the low center of gravity, helped by low placement of the 239ci engine. The owner is Palmer Fossum.

Chapter Four

Variations on the Jubilee

By the year 1955, the full impact of the new brand of management at Ford was being felt. It was now ten years since Henry Ford had turned over the reins to his grandson. The whiz kids that young Henry had brought in were changing everything. The "any-color-as-long-as-its-black" policy of Henry Ford, Sr. was discarded.

For the 1955 model year, two tractors were in the line-up: the Model 600 (134cid) and the Model 800 (172cid). There were three variations of the 600 designated the 640, 650, and 660. The more powerful Model 800, which was Ford's first U.S.-built three-plow tractor, was available as the 850 and 860. All versions were of the utility-tractor configuration, and all were equipped with live hydraulics and a three-point hitch. The model designations signified transmission and PTO configurations. The 640, 650, and 850 had transmission (non-live) PTOs while the 660 and 860 had live PTOs. The Model 640 had the four-speed transmission of the Jubilee; the others had a new five-speed transmission. The tractors were the same size

A Ford 650 built in 1956 in the foreground, with an incorrectly painted gray and blue 600 series behind it (the body panels should be grey, the transmission and axles should be red). The hundred series tractors were often painted blue by Ford dealers. Palmer Fossum's sharp "Lester" buildings, which house the Ford restoration business, are visible in the background.

Left: A Ford 650 showing the three-point hitch, a copy of the design by Harry Ferguson, with its Ford hydraulic touch control. The tractor photographed outside Palmer Fossum's Ford restoration workshops.

and shape as the Jubilee, but the 800s had larger tires and greater engine displacement.

In 1956, models proliferated with the 620 and 820 versions without PTO or three-point lift, and 630 version with lift but no PTO. These

A 1956 Ford 650 with the 600 series badge on the radiator.

Left: A 1956 Ford 650 with four-cylinder gasoline 134ci engine, five-speed transmission, non-live PTO, and three-point hitch. The owner is Palmer Fossum, Northfield, MN.

three "special utility" versions used the four-speed transmission. Also added were the 740, 950, and 960 "tricycle" versions. The 700 and 900 series were the same as the 600 and 800 except they were of the tricycle configuration. This line-up was then continued through 1957.

Palmer Fossum at the controls of his everyday 'contract work' tractor, a Ford 801 series

Powermaster. Powered by the Ford 172ci four-cylinder gasoline engine.

Before the end of the 1957 model year, the tractors of the Ford line were given a face lift and some improved features. To signify the im-provements, a "1" was added to each model designator, making, for example, the 640 into the 641. If the 134ci engine was used, the tractor

This 1958 Ford 861 cuts grass for the Cannon Falls School District in Minnesota. In the background is a Ford Jubilee.

A 1956 Ford 650 showing the four-cylinder overhead-valve 134ci gasoline engine. This Ford engine was introduced on the Jubilee in 1953 and produced 31bhp at 2000rpm.

was in the "Workmaster" series; if the 172ci engine was used, it was in the "Powermaster" series.

LPG (liquefied petroleum gas) variations of each engine were offered. Workmaster and Powermaster diesels became available in 1958 and 1959, respectively.

Two other additions occurred in 1959. The first was the 501 Workmaster series of high-crop off-set cultivating tractors. The second was the Se-

The 1953 Ford Golden Jubilee was an updated and revised 8N, built after Henry Ford's lawsuit with Harry Ferguson. Ford was forced to change the hydraulics from the Ferguson system to a Ford-designed pump that was mounted on the engine and driven by the camshaft.

A 1953 Ford Golden Jubilee with four-cylinder overhead-valve 134ci engine producing 31bhp at 2000rpm.

Left: The 1953 Ford Golden Jubilee badge on the radiator shroud commemorated the 50th anniversary of the founding of the Ford Motor Company in 1903.

lect-O-Speed power-shift planetary transmission providing ten forward speeds and two in reverse.

For all of its marketing effort to provide a multitude of models, Ford lost market share and U.S. production dropped below that of Ford, U.K., in 1956. This trend was to continue until the end of Fordson production in 1964. In some of these years, English production was triple that of American.

The only difference between the 1953 and 1954 Ford Jubilee was the revised medallion on the 1954, which doesn't have Golden Jubilee model 1903-1953 on it.

A Ford Jubilee with owner and restorer John Davis at the controls. John collects Case tractors and is from Maplewood, Ohio. Notice how the carburetor side of the 134ci engine is packed tight with inlet and exhaust manifolds and the horizontal muffler under the hood.

In 1959, the color scheme for the Workmaster line was changed to all red, with gray trim. The Powermaster line continued the red cast iron and gray sheet metal but added a red hood center strip and red grill.

There was a method to all of the model numbers that were available in this series. The following list shows how it all played out. For

A Ford Jubilee with 134ci four-cylinder gasoline engine, producing 31bhp at 2000rpm. The owner is John Davis of Maplewood, Ohio.

Right: The 1953 Ford Golden Jubilee was fitted with a brand new engine called the Ford Red Tiger. The 134ci four-cylinder engine had a compression ratio of 6.6:1 that produced 31hp at 2000rpm.

example, a Model 651 would signify a four-wheel utility tractor with a 134ci gasoline or 144ci diesel engine, a five-speed transmission, a live PTO, and a three-point hitch.

First Number

Number	Configuration
5xx	One-row, 8in offset design equipped with 134ci gasoline, LPG, or 144ci four-cylinder diesel.
6xx	Four-wheel utility type, with adjustable front axle. Equipped with 134ci gasoline, LPG or 144ci diesel.
7xx	High clearance row-crop type equipped with 134ci gasoline, LPG or 144ci four-cylinder diesel.
8xx	Four-wheel utility type with adjustable front axle. Equipped with 172ci gasoline, LPG or diesel engine.
9xx	High clearance row-crop type. Equipped with 172ci gasoline, LPG or diesel engine.

Middle Number

x1x	Select-O-Speed transmission without PTO.
x2x	Four-speed transmission, no PTO or three-point hitch.
x3x	Four-speed transmission without PTO.
x4x	Four-speed transmission with PTO and three-point hitch.

A 1954 Ford Jubilee NAA with mid-mounted grass cutter. This NAA is painted in the later post-1960 Ford blue.

Number	Configuration
x5x	Five-speed transmission, non-live PTO, three-point hitch.
x6x	Five-speed transmission, live PTO and three-point hitch.
x7x	Select-O-Speed transmission, single-speed PTO, three-point hitch.
x8x	Select-O-Speed transmission, with two-speed live and ground-drive (non-live) PTO. Three-point hitch.

Last Number

xx0	Built between 1955 and 1958.
xx1	Built between 1958 and 1961.

Additional Numbers and Letters

xxx-1	Tricycle type with single front wheel.
xxx-4	High-clearance four-wheel adjustable.
xxx-L	LPG engine.
xxx-D	Diesel engine.

A Ford 861 not long after proud owner Don
Alstad completed the restoration.

A 1958 Ford 861 beautifully restored by owner Don Alstad with help from Palmer Fossum and painted by Tim Alberg from Northfield, MN.

The 801 series was in production from 1958 until 1961.

A 1958 Ford 861 with live hydraulics and a three-point Ford hitch system. The 800 series was Ford's first U.S.-built three-plow tractor.

Right: A Ford 861 with red and gray radiator surround and hood. The large Ford hood emblem, similar to the older type on the Jubilee, is a difficult and expensive item to replace.

Left: A 1958 Ford 861 with gasoline 172ci engine, five-speed transmission, live PTO, and three-point hitch. The working weight is about 6900lbs for this three-plow tractor. Despite the choice and range of the hundred and hundred and one series, Ford lost their market share in the United States. The 500, 600, 700, 800, and 900 tractors were good tractors, but the competition was stiff in the late fifties.

A 1958 Ford 861. The four-cylinder overhead-valve 172ci gasoline engine has a bore and stroke of 3.9in and 3.6in producing 50hp at the belt. This one is owned and was restored by Don Alstad of Roseville, MN.

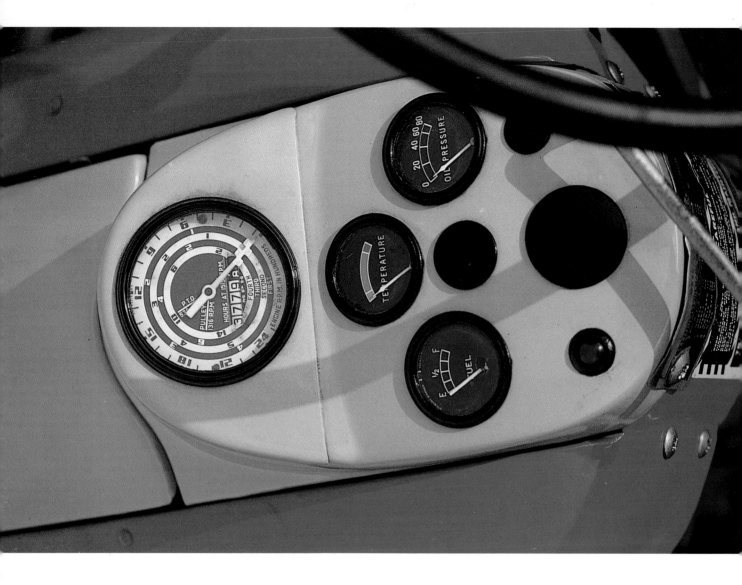

A 1958 Ford 501 Offset Workmaster instrument panel. The 501 series was painted the same colors as the 801 series, but the scheme was reversed. The 500 and 600 used the 134ci gasoline or 144ci diesel four-cylinder engines.

A 1958 Ford 861. The complicated side of the 172ci gasoline engine with carburetor, inlet manifold, muffler, and air filter all under the hood. The 860 was rated at 45hp at the belt, the 861 at 50hp at the belt and 43hp at the drawbar. The extra 5bhp of the 861 increases fuel consumption over it's predecessor.

Chapter Five

Modern Ford Tractors

In March of 1961, Ford Tractor Operations was established to coordinate the U.S. activities with those of Ford Motor Company Limited (U.K.). This was the first step in the plan to eliminating competition between U.S.- and U.K.-built tractors.

Also in 1961, the new six-cylinder Model 6000 was introduced. At about the same time, the model designations of the industrial line was changed to be consistent with the new 6000. The color scheme was changed to red-trimmed yellow. In early 1962, the number designations of the agricultural tractors were also changed to the four-digit scheme.

Agricultural and industrial model tractor numbers consisted of five digits, in some cases followed by a letter or a number. The following list shows how it worked out.

2xxx	Indicates a 134ci gas engine, or a 144ci diesel.
4xxx	Indicates a 172ci gas, LPG, or diesel engine.
x0xx	Industrial models prior to 1963.

A 1993 Ford 8730 'power shift' two-wheel-drive tractor equipped with a 401ci six-cylinder turbo-diesel engine that produces 140hp at the PTO. The optional 'Ultra-Command' power-shift transmission has eighteen forward and nine reverse gears.

x1xx	Industrial and agricultural models after 1963.
xx10	Row-crop.
xx11	Offset.
xx20	Utility type, adjustable front axle.
xx21	Orchard type, non-adjustable front axle.
xx31	Low center of gravity (LCG) type.
xx41	Heavy duty industrial, stub frame/cast grille.
x1x0	Four-speed, no PTO.
x0x1	Four-speed, no PTO or hydraulics.
x1x1	Four-speed with PTO.
x0x2	Four-speed with hydraulics, no PTO.
x1x2	Five-speed with live PTO.
x0x3	Four-speed with hydraulics and PTO.
x0x4	Select-O-Speed without hydraulics or PTO.
x1x4	Select-O-Speed without PTO.
x0x5	Select-O-Speed with hydraulics and 540rpm PTO.
x0x6	Select-O-Speed with hydraulics, 540 and 1000rpm and ground-speed PTO.
x1x6	Select-O-Speed with 540 and 1000rpm independent PTO.
x1x7	Select-O-Speed with 540 and 1000 rpm independent and ground-speed PTO.

A Ford TW15 series two with six-cylinder turbocharged diesel engine that produced 132hp. The tractor is cutting grass for silage with a John Deere alongside collecting grass. The TW15 series was built from 1986 until 1989.

Suffix letters and numbers signify the following:

xxxx-1   Tricycle type with a single front wheel.

xxxx-4   High clearance, four-wheel, adjustable front axle.

xxxx-D   Diesel engine.

xxxx-L   LPG engine.

To further eliminate competition between company divisions and to fill out the product line, the Fordson Super Major was given the Ford 5000 designation while the Super Dexta was called the Ford 2000 Diesel. This was a stop-gap measure to carry them over until the "World Tractors" could be readied. The paint combinations

This 1987 Ford TW15 has logged over 11,000 hours of work at the Bliss family farm near Kingsweston, Somerset, Great Britain. The tractor suffered one major mechanical disaster at 6,000 hours when the viscous-coupled fan jammed and the engine overheated and seized. The result was a new short block at $5,500. Despite the Bliss family's bad luck with this tractor, the TW15 is probably the best Ford tractor built.

were also changed so that all tractors were painted in variations of blue and gray, rather than red and gray (domestic) and blue and orange (U.K.).

In 1964, tractor production ended at Dagenham after thirty-one years, and with it, the end of the Fordson name. A new tractor plant was opened in Basildon, England. Concurrently, the Tractor Division converted the Antwerp, Belgium, plant to tractor production, and a plant was opened in Brazil.

A Ford TW15 with 132hp six-cylinder turbocharged diesel engine with sixteen manual forward speeds and four reverse speeds. The engine is rated at 121hp at the PTO.

Right: A 1990 Ford 5610 powered by a four-cylinder 256ci diesel producing 62hp at the PTO. The standard transmission has eight forward speeds. Sixteen-speed dual-power and synchromesh transmissions are optional.

The first new four-digit tractor, the Model 6000, did not fit into the concept of the World Tractor, since it was introduced in 1961 before things got organized.

The Model 6000

The Model 6000 was available in either gasoline, diesel, or LPG versions; the gasoline and LPG versions were 233cid while the diesel was 242cid. All developed a nominal 65hp. The ten-speed Select-O-Speed transmission was standard equipment for this 7000lb tractor. For

A Ford-Versatile 976 articulated four-wheel-drive tractor. The 350hp six-cylinder turbo- **diesel Cummins is mated to a dual-range twelve-speed transmission.**

1965, it was called the Commander 6000. It was built only in the U.S. and sold in the U.S., Canada, and Australia. The Model 6000 was Ford's first six-cylinder tractor, and its only one at the time of its introduction. After 1965, it was Ford's only row crop tractor; that is, the only one available with the dual-wheel tricycle front end. A wide-front was also available.

The Model 6000 was produced through the 1967 model year.

The Models 2000 through 5000

These models were first introduced in 1962 as merely a number change from the previous 600 and 800 series. The diesel 2000, prior to 1965, was either the English Fordson Dexta import or a 144ci four-cylinder version of the old Model 600. The Model 4000, nee 800, was available in diesel, gasoline, or LPG versions. The 5000 was the imported Fordson Super Major.

For 1965, the entire line, except for the 6000, received a complete redesign. The concept of the "World Tractor" was now in place.

Row-crop and offset tractors were eliminated from the line (except for the row-crop 6000). Innovative new three-cylinder engines replaced the four-cylinder units in the 2000-4000 series. The Model 5000 got a four-cylinder derivation of the new engine. All were available in either gasoline or diesel versions.

The new tractors were much more like the Dexta and Super Major than they were like the 600/800 Jubilee derivatives. In fact, outside the U.S., the 2000 was known as the Dexta 2000, and the 5000 was called the Super Major 5000.

The 2000 through 5000 tractors were produced through 1975. The Model 6000 was terminated in 1967.

Models 7000 Through 9000

Introduced early in 1968, the 8000 was a big tractor in any league. It used a 401ci six-cylinder diesel engine developing 105 PTOhp and was the first Ford to break the 100 horse-

A 1992 Ford-Versatile 976 built by the Versatile Farm Equipment Company of Winnipeg, Canada. Powered by a 350bhp 855ci Cummins NTA855 turbo-diesel six-cylinder.

A Ford-Versatile 976 designation 'S' with Brian Breken of Dennison, Minnesota, at the controls. The 900 series Versatile has a 130in wheelbase.

A Ford-Versatile 976 plowing. The smoke pouring from the exhaust pipe of the six-cylinder Cummins turbo-diesel producing is quite normal under full load.

power barrier. It weighed about 11,000 pounds and was rated for seven-plow bottoms in most soils. Styling of the new 8000 was reflected in the smaller Ford tractors for 1968, as well. It was the first Ford tractor to be routinely offered with a fully enclosed cab.

The Model 9000, known as "The Blue Brute," was introduced for the 1970 model year. It was the largest, most powerful Ford tractor up to that time. Normally weighing about 12,000 pounds, working weight (with ballast) could approach 18,000 pounds. The engine was a turbocharged version of the 8000's six-cylinder 401ci diesel. The 9000 was more than just a turbocharged 8000, however. It featured a heavier powertrain, larger radiator, and oil-cooled pistons. The engine was rated at 130hp.

A 1993 Ford-Versatile 876 Cummins turbo-diesel. This model was the last of the 800/900 series Versatiles with exposed engines. The 1994 eighty-series Versatiles have covered engines and more rounded Ford-New Holland styling.

Introduced in late 1971, the Model 7000 came later than the 8000 and 9000 in the grand scheme of things. Rated at 84hp, this 6200lb tractor used a four-cylinder 256ci turbocharged diesel engine. While most 7000s were of the utility configuration, row-crop configurations were also available for the first time in Ford tractors since the demise of the Model 6000 in 1967.

The 7000 was the first Ford to use the Load Monitor; a sophisticated electro-hydraulic replacement for Harry Ferguson's draft control spring. It sensed driveline torque and adjusted implement depth accordingly. This feature was later incorporated on other Ford tractors, as well.

The Models 1000 Through 1900

The Model 1000 was introduced in 1973 especially for the part-time farmer. It was powered by a 23hp two-cylinder diesel engine of 78cid. It

A 1973 Ford 8600 with the 401ci six-cylinder diesel engine that produces 110hp. The 401ci Ford diesel engine first appeared in the 8000 series in 1968 and was the first Ford engine to break the 100hp barrier. A longer stroke version of the same engine powers the larger Ford Tractors today.

weighed 2,600lb and was built for Ford by Ishikawajima Harima Industries in Japan.

For the 1977 model year, Ford Tractor Operations announced the Model 1600. It was essentially the same as the 1000, except for sheet metal changes to agree with the restyling of the line. In 1979, this tractor was again restyled and renumbered the Model 1700.

The Model 1900, also from Japan, was also introduced in 1979. It featured a three-cylinder diesel engine of 87cid. Its basic weight was just under 3,000lb.

Modern Variations

From 1975 and on, the Ford Motor Company, Tractor and Implement Division, now headquartered in Troy, Michigan, produced a truly competitive line of tractors. The line was maturing. All horsepower and weight classes were covered. Competitive positioning was

A Ford 4000 equipped with a diesel three-cylinder engine that produces 45hp at the PTO.

This 201ci Ford diesel engine has a bore of 4.4in and stroke of 4.4in.

now in the form of features, such as cabs, controls, and instrumentation. The basic powertrains did not change much from year to year. For the most part, tractors were grouped into series for marketing purposes.

The 600 Series
The Model 2600

Restyled and updated, this model replaced the 2000 in 1975. Engine improvements resulted in a slight increase in power. A fully-enclosed cab

was offered. Otherwise, the tractor was equipped with a ROPS (roll-over protection system).

The Model 3600

The 3600 was the 1975 styling version of the Model 3000. As with the 2600, six- and eight-speed manual transmissions were options. A cab was offered.

The Model 4600

Available only in the 201ci version for 1975,

the 4600 diesel was rated at 52hp, rather than at 45hp as in the Model 4000. The sheet metal was new for 1975. To fill the 45hp gap, a new model, the 4100 was introduced. It was the same as the 4600, except it used a 183ci diesel engine.

The Model 5600

Available with the four-cylinder 233ci diesel engine only, the 5600 replaced the 5000 in 1975. Engine improvements resulted in a 5hp increase to a rating of 60hp at the PTO. The transmission featured eight speeds plus partial range power shifting, which is essentially a two-range transmission that can be shifted on the fly.

The Model 6600

A new model introduced in 1975 to replace the old Commander 6000, the 6600 was a 7,000lb tractor with a four-cylinder 255ci diesel engine which produced a PTO rating of a nominal 70hp.

The Model 7600

The 1975 replacement for the Model 7000, this tractor used the same 255ci engine of the 6600, except that it was turbocharged and rated at 85hp.

The Model 8600

For 1973, the 105hp Model 8000 was replaced by the 110hp Model 8600. The power increase was the result of engine improvements, as the 401ci displacement and rated RPM were the same. The 8600 was available with a conventional front axle or with a set-back tricycle front end.

The Model 9600

The turbocharged 401ci diesel was upgraded to 135hp for this 1973 model that replaced the 9000. This model and its companion, the Model 8600, had nine square foot operator platforms and could be equipped with Ford's Tudor cab (a name borrowed from pre-1962 two-door automobiles).

The 700 Series

To celebrate the sixtieth anniversary of Ford tractors, the 700 Series was introduced in 1977.

The Model 6700

Reconfigured and restyled for 1977, the 6700 was now a platform tractor. Mechanically, it was the same as the previous 6600 model.

The Model 7700

Like the 6700 previously described, the 7700 was also now a platform tractor. The running gear was the same as for the Model 7600.

The Model 8700

Like the others in the 1977 line, the Model 8700 featured the new wraparound grille in flat black with a forward slanting nose. Otherwise, the 8700 was much like the 8600.

The Model 9700

The "Big Daddy" of two-wheel drive Ford tractors, the 9700 received the same face-lift as the 8700. Other features of the senior 700 Series tractors were upper pivoted pedals and separate pumps for implement lift and power steering.

The FW Series Four-Wheel Drives
The Model FW-20

In late 1977, Ford entered into an agreement with Steiger Tractor, Inc., to market a line of four-wheel drive super tractors built

by Steiger. Steiger, a pioneer in this field, also supplied such tractors to International Harvester and to their own dealers. The FW-20 employed a Cummins 210hp V-8 diesel engine of 555ci. The fixed-ratio transmission had twenty forward speeds. Working weight, with eight 23.1-30 tires, was 31,000 pounds.

A Ford 7810 series three Silver Jubilee with front-wheel assist (FWA) and limited-slip differential. Ford claims the FWA reduces fuel consumption by up to twenty percent.

equipped with a hydrostatic PTO that provided a maximum of 105hp. The FW-30 weighed about 1,000 pounds more than the FW-20.

The Model FW-40

Again, this tractor was basically the same as the FW-30 but with the Cummins 903ci engine producing 227hp at the drawbar.

The Model FW-60

The same tractor as the FW-40 but with turbocharging. The Cummins 903ci V-8 engine was rated at 335hp, and it produced a maximum drawbar horsepower of 271. The FW-60 weighed 34,000lb.

The TW Series

The Models TW-10 and TW-20 were updated replacements for the 8700 and 9700. Mechanical features remained the same, but the styling was upgraded to match the rest of the 1979 models. The Model TW-30 was the same as the TW-20, but an intercooler was added to the turbocharger brining the PTO horsepower up to 160. These models were again restyled for 1984 and redesignated the TW-5, TW-15, and TW-35. A new model was added; the TW-25, which was essentially the same as the TW-15, except the engine was rated at 140hp.

The 10 Series

In 1982, a new design scheme was introduced. Over the next two years, it was applied

The Model FW-30

Essentially the same as the FW-20, except for a 903ci Cummins V-8, the FW-30 had a maximum drawbar horsepower of 205. It was

This Ford 7810 series three uses the 401ci six-cylinder diesel engine. This Ford tractor—with it's smooth six-cylinder 100hp diesel—proved more popular than the 7710 equipped with an 86hp four-cylinder turbo-diesel. The standard equipment of the Silver Jubilee 7810 included many extras as such as air conditioning.

to the entire line. To the previous designations, a 10 was added. While most of the changes were superficial, the highlights are summarized in the following charts. Note that all Ford tractors were diesels by this time.

Model	Year	Hp	Cyl.	ci
1510	1983	20	3	68
1710	1983	24	3	85
1910	1983	28	3	104

These three were made for Ford by Ishi-kawajima-Shibaura Machinery Company of Tokyo, Japan. All had three-cylinder diesels, rather than the two-cylinder engines used in the smaller tractors. The engine in the 1910 had a longer stroke than that of the 1900. All had twelve-speed transmissions.

Model	Year	Hp	Cyl.	ci
2110	1984	35	4	136

This was a new model from Japan in 1984 and is not to be confused with the old 2000 designation, which has, by this time, become the 2910. The 2110 had a four-cylinder diesel of 139cid. Maximum PTO horsepower was 35. It was equipped with a twelve-speed transmission The basic weight of the 2110 was 3600 pounds. This compact tractor was made for Ford by Ishikawajima-Shibaura Machinery Company of Tokyo, Japan.

A Ford 7810 Silver Jubilee showing special silver and blue colors, with the air filter bowl protruding through the hood. The 401ci six-cylinder diesel has a bore of 4.4in and a stroke of 4.4in.

Right: The Ford 7810 is equipped with a six-cylinder diesel engine that produces 100hp at 2100rpm, 90hp at the PTO at 1,000rpm, and 87.2hp at the PTO at only 540rpm. The series three 7810 was one of the best-selling 100hp Ford tractors in Europe.

Model	Year	Hp	Cyl.	ci
2610	1982	37	3	175
2910	1984	37	3	175

The 2610 was an upgrade of the Model 2600 brought out in 1975. The stroke was lengthened to increase displacement from 158ci to 175ci. The Model 2910 was new for 1984. It was slightly heavier than the 2610, and it had larger tires. It was an upgrade of the old Model 2000.

Model	Year	Hp	Cyl.	ci
3610	1982	42	3	192
3910	1984	42	3	192
4610	1982	50	3	201

The 3910 is much the same as the 3610 except it is somewhat heavier.

Model	Year	Hp	Cyl.	ci
5610	1982	62	4	256
6610	1982	72	4	268
7610	1982	87	4	268 turbo

These are Ford's all-purpose four-cylinder tractors. They are carried up to the current model year, albeit in much improved form. The line was upgraded in 1994, and an "S" was added to the model name to signify an upgraded model. Displacements have increased, as well, as follows:

Model	Year	Hp	Cyl.	ci
5610S	1994	66	4	268

6610S	1994	76	4	304
7610S	1994	87	4	304 turbo

The 30 Series
The Models 3230 and 3430

These models, introduced in 1990, superseded similar ones in the 10 series. Both were equipped with three-cylinder diesels of 192cid, rated at 32hp and 38hp, respectively. The 3430 was available with a cab or in a low-center-of-gravity configuration.

For 1992, a Model 3415 was added. This was a less deluxe version, but it had an improved lift system and improved maintenance features.

The Models 3930 and 4630

Superseding the 3910 and 4610 in 1990, these two tractors were powered by three-cylinder diesels of 210ci. They were rated at 45hp and 55hp, respectively. The 4630 is available in a low-center-of-gravity version designed primarily for mowing on hilly terrain. Wheel settings as wide as seventy-eight inches are available.

The Models 8630, 8730, and 8830

These models replaced the TW Series in 1990. All used the 401ci turbocharged diesel engine, but the engine in the 8830 used an intercooler. Horsepower ratings were 121, 140, and 170.

Electronic performance monitoring was an option, giving a readout of wheel slip, ground speed, and acres per hour. The unit was operated by an onboard computer and a radar unit. A cab was standard.

The Powerstar Series

Introduced for 1993, the Powerstar Series represents the absolute latest and finest in agricultural tractors. Comfort Command cabs and implement performance instrumentation are options, as is four-wheel drive. Transmission options include the eight-speed manual, the eight-speed with partial range powershift, and two new shuttle transmissions that can be operated forwards or backwards in each of either six or eight gears. This is plus the partial-range powershift, for twelve or sixteen speeds in either direction. Characteristics of the Powerstars follow:

Model	Cyl.	Hp	ci	Weight
5640	4	66	268	7100
6640	4	76	304	7100
7740	4	86	304	7132
7840	6	90	401	8076
8240	6	96	456	8684
8340	6	112	456	8684

The 20 Series

The model year 1993 witnessed an upgrade of the Ishikawajima-Shibaura-built tractor line. The previous designations were changed from ten to twenty for this series of compact tractors, and 1215 and 1715 economy models were added.

Model	Cyl.	Hp	ci	Weight
1215	3	14	54	1300
1220	3	16	58	1375
1320	3	19	77	2150
1520	3	22	81	2200
1620	3	26	81	2300
1715	3	26	81	2000
1720	3	27	91	2550
1920	4	32	121	2900
2120	4	40	138	3675

A 1983 Ford 6610 with Chris Keen in the cab. Sam Lock is also shown with his Ford tractor. The 6610 has a 268ci four-cylinder diesel which produces 72hp at the PTO. The Sanderson 247TS Teleporter loader behind is loading seeds.

The Versatile Fords

In 1989, Ford bought the Versatile Farm Equipment Company of Winnipeg, Manitoba. It continued production of their line of articulated four-wheel drive tractors, with refinements and some number changes. The model

A Ford and Fordson sign in the corporate
colors of the thirties and forties. The colors
changed in the early fifties with the Jubilee and
new Majors.

Left: A 1995 Ford 8340 with 456ci six-cylinder
diesel engine producing 120hp at 2100rpm and
108hp at the PTO 9x 1000 rpm. The standard
transmission has twelve forward and twelve
reverse speeds with 'Synchro Shift' while the
'Electro Shift' has twenty-four forward and
twenty-four reverse speeds. The front PTO is
driven by the engine crankshaft. A LELY
Power harrowing drill is mounted on the rear.

numbers included 846, 876, 946, 976, and the
behemoth 1156. The latter used the Cummins
six-cylinder turbocharged and intercooled
1150ci diesel. This tractor, which had a working weight of 46,500lb, recorded a maximum
drawbar pull of 43,219lb. The "smaller" models use the Cummins 855ci six-cylinder diesel.
In the Model 976, it is rated at 350hp.

The Genesis 70 Series

The 145 to 210hp 70 series tractors are
new for 1994. The 8670, 8770, 8870, and 8970
replace the 8630, 8730, and 8830. They feature optional SuperSteer four-wheel drive row
crop front axles that reduce the turning circle
by forty percent, quiet two-door cabs, sixteen-
speed pulse shift powershift transmissions, an
optional 55gpm MegaFlow hydraulic system
with two pumps, and a movable "Side-
winder" control console that is easily posi-
tioned for the operator's personal conve-
nience.

All of the 70 series engines are six-cylinder
units of 456ci that are turbocharged. The 8870
and 8970 have intercoolers.

A 1995 Model Ford 8970 with the hood up to show the ease of servicing. This is the largest seventy series and is equipped with a 456ci six-cylinder turbocharged intercooled diesel which produces 240hp at 2100rpm with 225hp at the PTO. The transmission features eighteen forward and nine reverse speeds with clutchless shifting that is fully automatic in tenth gear or higher when the transmission is in automatic mode. A nice feature is the super steer front axle that dramatically reduces the tractor's turning radius by allowing the front wheels to turn a full 65degrees.

Horsepower ratings are as follows:

8670	145hp
8770	160hp
8870	180hp
8970	210hp

The new Genesis engines provide up to fifty percent torque backup, which is a measure of lugging power. Average torque backup is about thirty-five percent. The Genesis diesel engines achieve a remarkable maximum economy specific fuel consumption of 0.331lb of fuel per horsepower hour .

The SuperSteer Axle front wheel drive system actually shifts the front axle left or right. It is moved in the direction the wheels are turned. This is done to provide clearance between the front wheel and the frame when the wheel is cramped to the extreme angle. Thus the Genesis four-wheel drive tractors can turn much shorter the their competition.

The Genesis 70 Series tractors are built in the Canadian Versatile plant.

A Fiatagri F140 equipped with 358ci six-cylinder turbo-diesel which produces 140hp at 2250rpm. The standard transmission has twelve forward and twelve reverse gears. The optional Hi-Lo Creeper transmission has forty-eight forward and twenty-four reverse speeds. This 1995 model keeps the Fiatagri name in Europe though the company name is New Holland, with headquarters in Turin, Italy. In 1986, the Ford Motor Company had acquired Sperry-New Holland and called the new company Ford-New Holland. Fiat acquired Ford-New Holland in 1991 and named the merged company N.H. Geotech. In 1993, N.H. Geotech changed its name to New Holland. Today, New Holland has factories in Brazil, Belgium, Canada, France, India, Italy, Mexico, Pakistan, the United Kingdom, and the United States. The roots of the company are deep and diverse, stemming from companies like Braud, a French company founded in 1870; Laverda, an Italian company founded in 1873; New Holland, an American company founded in 1895; and Ford, the American company founded by Henry Ford in Detroit in 1903.

Epilogue

In 1991, the New Holland Holding Company was formed. The assets of Ford-New Holland and Fiat-geotech were placed under it's control. Ford owned twenty percent of the holding company and Fiat owned eighty percent. In 1992, Fiat, through a $600 million infusion of cash, increased its share to eighty-eight percent. Fiat's share has now increased to 100 percent. At some time in the near future, the Ford name will be dropped, and all products will be labeled "New Holland."

Recommended Reading

The following books offered essential background on the Ford tractors covered in this book. These make good library additions for any tractor buff. Most are available from Motorbooks International, P.O. Box 2, 729 Prospect Avenue, Osceola, Wisconsin 54020 USA. (800) 826-6600.

The Agricultural Tractor 1855-1950, by R.B. Gray, Society of Agricultural Engineers; an outstanding and complete photo history of the origin and development of the tractor.

The American Farm Tractor, by Randy Leffingwell, Motorbooks International; a full-color hardback history of all the great American tractor makes, including Ford.

The American Ford, by Lorin Sorensen, Motorbooks International (reprint); a word and picture story of Henry Ford, his company and its products.

The Century of the Reaper, by Cyrus McCormick, Houghton Mifflin Company; a first-hand account of the Harvester and Tractor Wars by the grandson of the inventor.

The Development of American Agriculture, by Willard W. Cochrane, University of Minnesota Press; an analytical history.

Farm Tractors 1926-1956, Randy Stephens, Editor, Intertec Publishing; a compilation of pages from The Cooperative Tractor Catalog and the Red Tractor Book.

Fordson, Farmall and Poppin' Johnny, by Robert C. Williams, University of Illinois Press; a history of the farm tractor and its impact on America.

Ford Tractors, by Robert N. Pripps and Andrew Morland, Motorbooks International; a full-color history of the Fordson, Ford-Ferguson, Ferguson, and Ford tractors, covering the influence these historic tractors had on the state of the art of tractor design.

Ford and Fordson Tractors, by Michael Williams, Blandford Press; a history of Henry Ford and his tractors, especially concentrating on the Fordson.

Ford Trucks Since 1905, by James K. Wagner, Crestline Publishing Company. This work includes all the important tractor events, as well.

Harvest Triumphant, by Merrill Denison, WM. Collins Sons & Company LTD; the story of human achievement in the development of agricultural tools, especially that in Canada, and the rise to prominence of Massey-Harris Ferguson (now known as the Verity Corporation). Rich in the romance of farm life in the last century and covering the early days of the Industrial Revolution.

How to Restore Your Farm Tractor, by Robert N. Pripps, Motorbooks International; follows two tractors through professional restoration; one a 1939 Ford-Ferguson. Includes tips, techniques , commentary and photos.

Threshers, by Robert N. Pripps and Andrew Morland, Motorbooks International; a color history of grain harvesting and threshing featuring photos and descriptions of many of the big threshers in operation, some including Ford tractors.

Young Henry Ford, by Sidney Olson, Wayne State University Press; a pictorial history of Ford's first forty years.

9N-2N-8N Newsletter, published by G.W. Rinaldi, Box 235 Chelsea, VT 05038-0235. Four information-packed issues per year. The newsletter now covers the 500–900 series, as well. It is essential for anyone interested in 1939 to 1961 Ford tractors.

Illustrated Ford & Fordson Tractor Buyer's Guide, by Robert N. Pripps, Motorbooks International; covers the full range of Ford, Fordson, and Ford-Ferguson tractors from 1917 to 1967. This guide is indispensable for the enthusiast who is buying, restoring, and collecting these tractors.

Index